Inspired Minds

*Educational Strategies
for
Underserved Students*

By
Jerome Bronson

Inspired Minds: Educational Strategies for Underserved Students
Published by Watersprings Publishing,
a division of Watersprings Media House, LLC.
P.O. Box 1284 Olive Branch, MS 38654

www.waterspringspublishing.com

Contact publisher for bulk orders and permission requests.

Copyright © 2022 Jerome Bronson. All rights reserved.

No part of this publication may be reproduced, distributed, or transmitted in any form or by any means, including photocopying, recording, or other electronic or mechanical methods, without the prior written permission of the publisher, except in the case of brief quotations embodied in critical reviews and certain other noncommercial uses permitted by copyright law.

Printed in the United States of America.

ISBN-13: 978-1-948877-95-4

CONTENTS

SECTION 1
Introduction. 1

SECTION 2
What is a Quality Education? 9

SECTION 3
Intrinsic Factors to Success. 19

SECTION 4
Addressing Systemic Racism in Education. 25

SECTION 5
Extrinsic Influencers 31

SECTION 6
Holistic Perspective of the Student. 37

SECTION 7
Parental Role in Academic Success 47

SECTION 8
Educational Strategies for Success 57

Author Bio 69

SECTION I

Introduction

As recently as 1985, the U.S. government finally acknowledged that health disparities of minorities existed with the release of the Heckler Report. Before 1985, the illnesses and causes of death of minorities were not recorded or studied. When a physician saw a black patient, they were given a survey during the check-in process. If the patient checked a box that their parents or grandparents had hypertension, diabetes, etc., then the doctor would inform the patient that because of heredity, they would probably have those same health issues, and that would be the end of the diagnosis. With only about 35 years of the health of minorities being recognized as a real thing in this country, we are light years behind in understanding how social determinants of health such as where we live, work, play, & worship impact the quality of life for minorities. Racism as a public health crisis highlights the correlation between health disparities and educational attainment as well as a threat to the physical and psychological well-being of minority populations. There is a direct relationship between poor health and lower educational attainment (level of education completion). Poor health, disabilities, and unhealthy behaviors play a significant role in educational outcomes and performance in the classroom.

Meaningful dialogue about the strengths and resiliency of the African American youth should always begin with an acknowledgment of the relenting barrage of structural and systemic barriers to upward mobility in life or improving their quality of life. It is important to mention the problems plaguing minority students, such as racism and inadequate access to quality education, not from a victim mentality but to garner attention to the strength and resiliency required to overcome obstacles. A heightened level of focus should be placed on the attributes or factors that allow many minorities to become resilient and successful in life. Resiliency cannot take place without some form of threat, risk, or adversity. Access to resources reduces the negative impact of the risk exposure or offsets the effect of risk by increasing internal motivation and developmental competency. An example of developmental competency would be learning from a mistake and not repeating that mistake. Thus, the critical importance of fully funding schools for some level of protection against societal risks such as racism, violence, and drugs in communities of color.

> We should all aspire to a worthy cause that is greater than ourselves.

That motivates us to get out of bed in the morning and be an agent of change. The social injustice in how underserved students are denied access to quality education in cities and towns around America is that cause for me. I choose to use my voice and platform to advocate for equity in public education. Every child deserves the opportunity to receive a high-quality education to increase their chances for success in life. Unfortunately, the education system is failing to meet the needs of students that need help to achieve academic success. The COVID-19 Pandemic shined a bright light on the severity of disparities in communities of color. Remote learning for the 2020-2021 school year was lost for many students in underserved communities with limited access to the internet, Wi-Fi, and many schools dropped the ball on providing equipment, such as laptops for students whose parents could not afford the needed devices. The technology component of learning will only increase in the years to come. Educational leaders must be prepared with the technology infrastructure to provide all students with the necessary learning tools. It requires a multifaceted approach to meet the needs of today's learners; the question is no longer are students ready but are the schools prepared to help students with the self-development process. Self-development is taking personal responsibility for one's own learning and development through a process of assessment, reflection, and taking action with real-world application of what one has learned. Self-development aims to achieve your full potential, whether in your professional or personal life. Thus, one of the aims of public education should be to develop the whole student. Including academics, well-being/ mental health, and social development so that students can grow into adults equipped to build relationships with people that may be different from them in some way. Social development requires removing barriers so that all citizens (students) can experience the journey to adulthood and pursue their passions and dreams with dignity.

Nearly 70 years after the Brown VS Board of Education ruling by the U.S. Supreme Court, our public education system in the U.S. remains separate and unequal. And many of the issues that people were hung, beaten, and brutalized for during the Civil Rights Movement in the 1950s & 1960s, we are back to fighting for, such as the right to vote and heavy burdens of systemic racism on the necks of people of color. We have enough research and studies on the issue of racism in America. We know where the problems lie, with the root of them being access, equity, and equal opportunities for people of color. Yet, we remain a nation that refuses to invest in the lives of minority youth, namely in denial of adequately funding public education. The federal government gives the responsibility to the states, and the states provide the bare minimum for poor communities. We are forced to accept the excuse that low tax revenue is the culprit of the lack of funding in our school systems. The disparities in education continue to the college level for those minorities that are fortunate enough to graduate college. The student loan industry continues to fatten its pockets with profits exceeding one trillion dollars annually. African Americans and Hispanics are twice as likely to be saddled with student loan debt as their white counterparts while attempting post-secondary education. With many minorities unable to repay their student loan debt, their credit rating takes a drastic negative hit. Subsequently, this subgroup of the population is denied a line of credit for home and automobile loans and is forced to purchase these essential items with a subprime loan with an interest rate near or above twenty percent.

As a first-generation college graduate and licensed educator in the state of Mississippi, I feel compelled to be an advocate for the total funding of the public education system in the U.S. We must invest in the lives of future leaders of this country with funding, adequate resources, and our time to increase the chances for all children to become successful adults. Being a product of a single-parent home and growing up in a small Mississippi Delta community, my perspective is one in which I overcame many of these same systemic barriers to a high-quality education that is impeding health, and social development so that students can grow into adults equipped to build relationships with people that may be different from them in some way. Social development requires removing barriers so that all citizens (students) can experience the journey to adulthood and pursue their passions and dreams with dignity.

Nearly 70 years after the Brown VS Board of Education ruling by the U.S. Supreme Court, our public education system in the U.S. remains separate and unequal. And many of the issues that people were hung, beaten, and brutalized for during the Civil Rights Movement in the 1950s & 1960s, we are back to fighting for, such as the right to vote and heavy burdens of systemic racism on the necks of people of color. We have enough research and studies on the issue of racism in America. We know where the problems lie, with the root of them being access, equity, and equal opportunities for people of color. Yet, we remain a nation that refuses to invest in the lives of minority youth, namely in denial of adequately funding public education. The federal government gives the responsibility to the states, and the states provide the bare minimum for poor communities. We are forced to accept the excuse that low tax revenue is the culprit of the lack of funding in our school systems. The disparities in education continue to the college level for those minorities that are fortunate enough to graduate college. The student loan industry continues to fatten its pockets with profits exceeding one trillion dollars annually. African Americans and Hispanics are twice as likely to be saddled with student loan debt as their white counterparts while attempting post-secondary education. With many minorities unable to repay their student loan debt, their credit rating takes a drastic negative hit. Subsequently, this subgroup of the population is denied a line of credit for home and automobile loans and is forced to purchase these essential items with a subprime loan with an interest rate near or above twenty percent.

As a first-generation college graduate and licensed educator in the state of Mississippi, I feel compelled to be an advocate for the total funding of the public education system in the U.S. We must invest in the lives of future leaders of this country with funding, adequate resources, and our time to increase the chances for all children to become successful adults. Being a product of a single-parent home and growing up in a small Mississippi Delta community, my perspective is one in which I overcame many of these same systemic barriers to a high-quality education that is impeding the future of many minority students. As a Doctor of Public Health candidate at Jackson State University, an HBCU (historically black colleges and universities), and Harvard University fellow, my academic accomplishments have inspired me to be on the front line for the fight to ensure that minorities have proper representation at the table in academia. One of the purposes of this book is to debunk the debate that minorities are less intelligent than whites, but, on the contrary, the difference lies in access, opportunity, and exposure to a high-quality education. I grew up poor, neither of my parents graduated high school, but I was blessed to witness my parents' strong work ethic and learned what hard work, dedication, and persistence can do for you.

The National Institute of Health is federally funded medical research with an annual budget of 41 billion dollars, and only 1% of this funding goes to black researchers and scientists. At the highest level in academia (doctorate & Ph.D.), minorities are underrepresented and excluded because of the racial biases of those determining who gets approved for these research grants. Thanks to the prestigious Jackson Heart Study, which was the largest longitudinal study of cardiovascular disease in African Americans, I can conduct cardiovascular disease research that is funded through NIH. More minorities deserve the exposure and opportunities to conduct scientific research. It is an atrocity that only one percent of highly qualified black researchers and scientists are allowed to pursue medical research in the United States. The exclusion of black researchers in medical research is a perfect example that access does not mean inclusion. I will continue to advocate for equity in academia at all levels, K-12, college, and graduate-level studies.

SECTION 2

What is a Quality Education?

Every student in America deserves the fundamental right to quality education. Although the U.S. constitution does not grant students the right to an adequate education, there's a correlation between educational attainment and the quality of life that a person can potentially have in the United States. A high-quality education provides students with the opportunity to reach their full potential in life with both knowledge and social skills to flourish as a member of society. Unfortunately, social injustice and systemic racism continue to be pervasive in schools across America. Eliminating barriers to adequate access to resources for academic achievement is a necessity in poor communities. Teachers in poorer communities are tasked with educating students with the bare minimum educational tools at their disposal. And many of the classrooms in these same communities have non-certified (licensed) teachers or teachers without the proper subject matter expertise.

In 2021, it still required a village to raise a child. Complete buy-in from all facets of society, including community members, local stakeholders, civic organizations, family, teachers, etc., to deliver the same message to the youth that they are uniquely special and can achieve greatness in life. Positive reinforcement uplifts and empowers self-confidence in our future leaders matriculating through the early stages of life into adolescence then young adulthood.

> Everyone that comes into contact with youth has a role to play in positively impacting their lives.

In communities of black and brown populations, adults must be intentional about speaking positivity into the lives of the youth. Living in blight or economically poor communities, the children have a plethora of lived experiences seeing hopelessness and seemingly no way out. Education remains a viable option for at-risk youth to change the trajectory of their lives by graduating high school and attending college. Increased levels of educational attainment provide the opportunity to those on the lower end of the social class to improve their social mobility. Just because a child is born into poverty does not mean that must be their lot in life. Education provides the lifeline to upward mobility in society.

Hosea 4:6 KJV lets us know, people perish for lack of knowledge. The educational system is failing to meet basic educational services for marginalized children. Hypothetically speaking, what if we leveled the playing field (quality educational opportunities) for all children in America. Each child had a nurturing learning environment, sufficient educational tools, and proper nourishment? I believe we would then see a drastic increase in educational outcomes regardless of the economic status of the community in which a child lives. Equity in education is a necessity for all children to succeed. America must address fully funding k-12 education to ensure that future generations have a chance to succeed in life.

The key to unlocking potential, gifts, or talents involves activating the inner belief in one's ability to accomplish the task that confronts them. There must be an unrelenting and resilient paradigm shift in the thought processes of students that are facing astronomical odds of repeating the generational influences of living life at a lower social class. At the lower social class level, education is often not the focal point of most households living at or below the poverty level. Making ends meet financially and struggling to keep the utilities in service and assuring the next meal on the table takes precedence in poor communities. The power to uplift, inspire and motivate at-risk youth allows these children to reimagine a brighter future. The influential value of a reimagined vision of success is worth trusting the process of being resilient and determined to overcome obstacles and barriers. As individuals, some of us can naturally tap into the inner drive to push through adversity, difficulties, and challenges by exercising the willpower or self-control to see it through or get to the victory side of the obstacle. Taking control of your thoughts, emotions, and actions will play an essential role in mastering winning habits. There is no way around becoming proficient in self-control and developing self-discipline; you must go through the process of exercising these habits. The ability to think critically and examine your actions or reasoning before execution go hand in hand with mastering your decision-making processes.

> Effective decision-making is a quality shared by most leaders.

Following the crowd or doing what everyone else does should never be a factor in your thought process, but instead, base your decisions on your convictions and belief system. Being true to yourself grants you access to the authority to stand your ground while gaining the strength to face challenges head-on and overcoming the fear of failure associated with unproductive results of not trying at all. You cannot succeed by always being passive, or taking a wait and see what happens attitude, being proactive, and taking charge by simply trusting yourself to make sound (good) decisions. The synergy produced by being proactive and going with your gut instinct or intuition will compel you to act or respond based on what you know about something.

Keys for student success is developing a solid foundation of learning and resiliency in students focusing on the things in their control. Study habits, perception of one's belief in their abilities, and commitment to making decisions that will positively impact their future. The decision-making process is a critical component in the overall development of youth. The goal is for youth to become well-rounded adults, knowledgeable, skilled, and flourishing members of society. The transition from adolescence to adulthood should manifest some attributes of a well-balanced life, with multi-faceted skills set, resourcefulness, accountability for one's actions, and resiliency. For students to evolve into influential adults, it requires developing self-discipline by setting and mastering goals through practice in the adolescent and young adult years. Setting goals requires a focus that teaches planning, strategizing, and execution or follows through. The follow-through provides the opportunity for young people to see a task or objective carried out to completion. Seeing a task, goal, or desire come to fruition deposits confidence in students that they can utilize later in life by recalling times when they accomplished a seemingly difficult task.

Students need to envision themselves successful and reimagine themselves as successful despite the repetitive, often oppressive experiences of living at or below the poverty level. Adults view it as paying dues in life, but how do we get young people to buy into the delayed gratification that comes from doing the right things in life consistently or at a mastery level and waiting for the fruits of their hard work and dedication. We live in a society where instant gratification is seemingly the norm. The long game of delayed gratification is achieved by harnessing the power of believing in oneself and tapping into the visualization of success.

> Students must see themselves as successful and should base their decisions on impacting their future success.

Making wise choices and decisions is like making deposits at the bank on a smaller scale. They are investments in the vision or future. But on a larger scale or perspective, making smart decisions teaches accountability and winning habits in life. It is not guaranteed that every at-risk youth will have an active role model in their lives. But, if we can train students to believe in themselves, set goals, chase their dreams, and thrive in life motivated by intrinsic factors, then maybe we can ensure that no student is left behind.

> It is never too early to begin setting goals and developing a sense of purpose in life.

A life lived with a purpose provides direction or trajectory for navigating the highs, lows, pitfalls, setbacks, and disappointments that are sure to come at some point during a person's lived experiences. Students need guidance to understand that life is similar to a roller coaster ride and that there will be highs and lows but staying true to their purpose or calling will allow them to remain focused on their goals when facing challenging times. Having core beliefs and principles by which a person strives to live helps keep a person anchored during the tough times. A purpose-filled life supersedes a complacent or status quo type of life which often results in individuals merely existing or living day to day coasting along with no clear direction on where they are going in life. A life of purpose surpasses a life of drifting or settling for whatever happens. Those core beliefs are beneficial to avoid drifting away from their purpose in life. Challenges or experiences produce a fight or flight response when the body faces a stressful situation. Some individuals choose to flee the challenge to elevate the stressful feelings, while others can resist the stressful sensation by choosing to overcome the challenge by going in attack mode to offset a stressful situation.

Debunking the notion that all minorities are less intelligent than other races and lazy creatures. Systemic racism denies many marginalized people opportunities and exposure. Racial biases are visible at the highest levels of academia. For example, the National Institute of Health (NIH) has an average annual budget of $40 billion for scientific/biomedical research. Much of this money is awarded to white researchers at predominantly white institutions of higher learning. Black scientists and researchers are awarded only about two percent of the annual funding. African Americans and other minorities deserve an opportunity to conduct scientific research. For the most part, minorities are excluded from the table in academia, unable to showcase their intellect and talent. This is a perfect example of a lack of opportunities; we can have the same level of education, academic success and still be denied an opportunity. Empowering and motivating youth to excel academically is necessary to ensure that future scholars are represented in academia and granted an opportunity to showcase their abilities as scholars. It is less about I.Q. or intelligence that separates the ability to learn but more about access to opportunities and exposure to quality programming in schools.

SECTION 3

Intrinsic Factors to Success

How do we develop a path to success for marginalized and at-risk students? Psychologist Albert Bandura proposed the concept of self-efficacy. He proposed that a person's belief in their abilities to succeed in a particular situation is self-efficacy. Bandura's theory on self-efficacy focused on four components, namely mastery experiences (performance outcomes), vicarious experiences (social role models), social persuasion (verbal feedback), and emotional and physiological states. Self-efficacy lays the groundwork for motivation, well-being, and personal accomplishment. Mastery experiences include tangible evidence that one can succeed at a particular task. The saying "practice makes perfect" reflects a person's ability to repeatedly have success at achieving goals. If you poll any great athlete, their explanation of how they became great will include a countless number of hours practicing their craft. With the accumulation of success in performing a particular task, an individual's self-efficacy begins to increase exponentially. The second component of self-efficacy is vicarious experiences or seeing someone like oneself achieving success.

> It is so important for marginalized students to see individuals from similar backgrounds succeeding in life.

Having that visual of someone similar provides motivation and hope that I, too, can have similar success. Social role models come in various forms, such as a family member, teacher, or someone in the local community. The third component of self-efficacy is social persuasion or feedback.

Self-efficacy is influenced by receiving positive feedback or affirmation that I can achieve success. Positive feedback encourages us in those unsure moments or when self-doubt creeps into our minds causing us to abort the challenge that we face. This is often manifested in the paralyzing fear of failure that prevents us from attempting to do something that we have never done before. The fourth component of self-efficacy is our emotional and physiological state. The ability to manage our emotional state of being is a critical aspect of self-efficacy. Our perception of ourselves and our abilities plays a significant role in determining the positive impact that can be leveraged by self-efficacy.

Self-efficacy allows us to evaluate the wholeness of students, including their physical and mental health. The holistic perspective delves into the healthy behaviors of the mind, body, and spirit and meets the needs of students both academically and socially. The influence of self-efficacy increases when a person perceives that they are succeeding in multiple areas of their lives. In the educational system, we have achieved the ability to access the learning abilities of students while failing to adequately address many of the social problems that plague under-represented populations. It is virtually impossible for students to freely focus on academic achievement while facing food insecurities at home or physical and mental abuse. It may be an unfair burden placed on school systems to identify and address the social challenges of at-risk students. Still, teachers and counselors are perfectly positioned to notice red flags in behavior changes that can potentially result from adverse conditions in the home. One of the many roles of teachers is observing their students, and school systems that are proactive in having mechanisms in place to address the social struggles of students and families is a key to increasing student success rates.

Intrinsic motivation vs. Self-efficacy

Motivation is based on an individual's desire to achieve a certain goal, while self-efficacy is based on an individual's belief in their capacity to achieve said goal. Distinguishing between motivation and self-efficacy is important in developing approaches that allow students to tap into their abilities to achieve success. Intrinsic motivation is the act of doing something without any obvious external rewards. A person does a particular task because of pure enjoyment or self-interest rather than an outside incentive or pressure to do so.

Peeling back the layers that separate motivation from self-efficacy reveals the possible triggers that ignite action. There is a need to understand what causes a person to act or attempt a task under various conditions. For example, self-motivated individuals may not require as much positive feedback or reinforcement from others to achieve success. In contrast, others may require exponential amounts of reassurance that they can accomplish a task before attempting to do so. Some individuals can overcome adverse circumstances and achieve great success. What are the intrinsic triggers that allow individuals to become resilient and relentless in their pursuit of achieving said goals? Self-efficacy and intrinsic motivation are predictors of success. Self-efficacy allows individuals to believe in their abilities to achieve, while intrinsic motivation is a desire to achieve. Although, in theory, self-efficacy and motivation are different, both terms are potential catalysts to achieving success.

SECTION 4

Addressing Systemic Racism in Education

Addressing Systemic Racism

Systemic racism includes the policies and practices that exclude minority groups from opportunities to thrive and succeed. Inequities in education are still prevalent due to a lack of funding and resources for marginalized people. The bulk of funding for K-12 education comes from the state and local government, and the amount of funding is predicated on the tax base of the community within which the school system lies. As a result, poor students are penalized for the economic conditions of their communities as well as the access to adequate resources that are often found in more affluent communities.

> "More federal funding is needed to improve the quality of education offered to marginalized students in the United States."

Increasing the funding for K-12 requires advocacy on the local, state, and national levels to move the conversation forward on making adequate education for all a reality.

It is hypocritical to assess and evaluate student performance outcomes while expecting minority students to achieve a level of success while denying the reality of a real lack of resources. Equity in education levels the playing field and provides all students the same opportunity and resources.

U.S. Public Education Spending Statistics

- K-12 schools spend **$612.7 billion annually** or **$12,612** per pupil.

- Federal, state, and local governments spend **$720.9 billion**, or **$14,840** per pupil, to fund K-12 public education.
- The federal government provides **7.7%** of funding for public education; state and local governments provide **46.7%** and **45.6%** of public education funds, respectively.
- The United States spends an average of **$15,908** per pupil on postsecondary education and **$33,063** per pupil on graduate and postgraduate education.
- The nation's gross domestic product (GDP) grows **71.6%** faster than public education spending. (www.educationdata.org)

Nuances of Access and Inclusion

Not addressing the barriers and systemic racism in education is a major force in preventing minority students from excelling academically. Many times, the terms equity and equality are used interchangeably, although they have different meanings. With equality, the focus is more on treating groups of people the same, while equity focuses on meeting the needs of the individual.

> **Equity in public education ensures that students receive the individualized tools/resources needed for success.**

With the prevalence of diversity and inclusion measures coming to the forefront, many students lack the access and opportunities to excel academically. For underrepresented students that are fortunate enough to gain access to a highly rated school, that is only half of the victory. The next point of emphasis is if those institutions have the mechanisms in place to meet the needs of minority students. Schools must have a social support system to meet the needs of students outside of the classroom. We must address the environmental risk factors that hinder the academic success of minority students. Food insecurities, stress, and nutrition are some of the risk factors disadvantaged students face while attempting to excel in the classroom. Equity in education is cognizant of the environmental factors facing at-risk students and the proper mechanisms in place to address some of the challenges confronting marginalized students.

Socioeconomic status (SES) is another predictor of academic success for students. Students from lower SES often struggle with learning or display behavior issues in school. Although it may be difficult to implement strategies to improve educational outcomes based on the SES of students, developing resources, or directing families to resources can potentially change the trajectory of a family's financial situation. Different components of SES, such as the parents' educational and income levels, are key predictors of how a student will perform academically.

SECTION 5

Extrinsic Influencers

Social Persuasion

The level of feedback that students receive from their teachers plays a significant role in improving performance outcomes. Positive feedback can increase student's belief in their abilities to achieve success in school. Often, schools are focused on evaluating and assessing students while neglecting to provide timely feedback on areas of strengths and weaknesses. With so much attention on state-mandated assessment tests, teachers are forced to use "teach to the test" methods to prepare students to pass these required tests. Teaching to the test is merely teaching students techniques to pass standardized tests and less focused on knowledge acquisition and retention.

Social Role Model

Vicarious experiences are those observations of others and the attempt to mimic a similar action. Under-represented students need to see and observe others from a similar background to leverage the power of motivation and perception of seeing oneself achieving similar successes. Vicarious experiences allow students to visualize themselves overcoming perceived obstacles and barriers to mastering a task or goal. Repetition of success with tasks increases one's perception of their abilities or affirms possible success. Unfortunately, many underrepresented students lack the exposure or interaction with someone that comes from a similar background that has ascertained a certain level of success in life. The impact of having someone from a similar background to relate to is important in developing self-efficacy and improving one's perception of their chances to succeed.

> Role modeling is a selfless act because it requires that we intentionally display healthy behavior for students to mimic.

Role modeling exposes our vulnerabilities, setbacks, and failures. Effective role models believe that the only failure is not trying or giving your best effort. You do not have to be great to start, but you have to get started to be great. In other words, we cannot achieve any task, mission, or goal without taking some form of action. After enduring the many challenges of systemic racism and overcoming barriers, the fortunate minorities that manage to achieve great success in life often do not look back to acknowledge the struggle because of the painful reminders of the trials and tribulations required to attain success but simply choose to exhale because they made it out. Individuals that are self-assured are not intimidated or afraid to share their experiences that led to success, and they are willing to coach others that are on a similar path. Every victory in life or open door that is accessed creates an opportunity to give someone a hand up or display reciprocity by recreating a path for future generations to experience similar success by sharing with younger people strategies to succeed and providing advice to avoid potential pitfalls.

We can choose our disposition on any matter, whether we choose to see the glass as half-full of optimism or half-empty with self-doubt and wavering on our abilities to accomplish anything. Failure and rejection are opportunities that are valuable experiences that allow us to build resilience and determination.

> We should not view failures as shameful, negative moments but as tools to equip the next generation of leaders on how to achieve success.

Falling in life is a great opportunity to gain an understanding of our strengths and weaknesses. Getting back up again after falling requires us to utilize strength to get back on our feet; this may be the strength that may be lying dormant or discovery of inner strength that we may not have known that we possess. Sharing is caring and sharing painful moments of rejection or failure, and being transparent are teachable moments on the importance of never giving up on yourself or a goal of yours.

Achieving greatness is not an easy task. We cannot shy away from the responsibility of sharing the highs and lows and disappointments in climbing the ladder of success. Trusting the process of exhibiting healthy behaviors and doing what is right are necessary for matriculating to adulthood. Ultimately, we as individuals can define what success looks like for our lives, and it may not be a monetary amount that is the ultimate goal. Living a purposeful life and setting and achieving personal goals is an example of what success looks like. Students need to hear that every day may not be easy but that living life with purpose means that even on the rough or dark days, progress is being made. The burden is too great to carry when allowing others to define success for us and living up to someone else's expectations or vision for your life. Instead, blaze your trail as you construct your vision for a successful and satisfying life.

We must be tenacious about overcoming barriers and personal adversity in life. One of the greatest basketball players of all time, Michael Jordan, was cut from the varsity basketball team the first time he tried out. He did not quit and give up on his desire to play basketball, but instead, he put in extra time practicing and working on his skills and tried again the next year. To achieve greatness, giving up should never be an option.

The relatability of role models increases the impact of the influence they can have on students. Just as Michael Jordan is a great example for aspiring athletes, children from underserved communities need to have interactions with minority doctors, lawyers, and other professionals to bolster the idea that an at-risk student can be the next great whatever they desire to be. Someone can deliver the same message of a different ethnic group, and then someone of the same ethnic group and the listener may receive those messages differently. It is easier to receive motivational or inspirational messages from someone of a similar background because of the perception that you possibly know how I feel or can relate due to similar adversities.

SECTION 6

Holistic Perspective of the Student

Emotional and Physiological State

The emotional, physical, and psychological well-being of a person are key indicators of how they perceive themselves. Academic achievement requires meeting the needs of the student from a holistic perspective. It can be hypocritical to expect students to focus on mastering a particular skill or produce prolific scores on an assessment test when they are worried about not having any food at home for dinner or arriving at school late and missing out on breakfast, which happens to be one of their guaranteed meals for the day. There is not enough focus on the stress and peer pressure that students are coping with regularly and seemingly no outlet valve to release the associated burdens. The older siblings in a single-family household are often saddled with parenting duties, such as being a caregiver to younger siblings after school. Filling the role of a parent after school for older siblings diminishes the amount of time they can adequately devote to homework or studying.

According to the CDC, healthy students are better learners, and academic achievement bears a lifetime of benefits for health. However, youth risk behaviors, such as physical inactivity, unhealthy dietary behaviors, tobacco use, alcohol use, and drug use, are consistently linked to poor grades and test scores and overall lower educational attainment. An emphasis on teaching and modeling healthy behaviors to students must be included in the curriculum. Mastery of healthy behaviors is equally as important as the core courses when developing a complete student. This will equip every student with the necessary tools to attain academic success. There is a direct correlation between health disparities and educational inequities. Social determinants of health (SDOH) are the conditions in the environments where people are born, live, work, play, worship, and age that affect a wide range of health, functioning, and quality of life outcomes and risks. Social determinants of health consist of five components: economic stability, educational access, and quality, healthcare access and quality, neighborhood and built environment, and social and community context.

According to Healthy People 2030, Children from low-income families, children with disabilities, and children who routinely experience social discrimination — like bullying — are more likely to struggle with math and reading. They're also less likely to graduate from high school or go to college. This means they're less likely to get safe, high-paying jobs and more likely to have health problems like heart disease, diabetes, and depression.

Addressing Mental Health

Acknowledgment that mental health plays an important role in the lives of adolescents and youth. The number of teenagers experiencing mental health issues is rising dramatically. Adolescents must be provided with coping mechanisms by professional counselors to safely handle stress, depression, and/or anxiety. Prevention strategies for behavioral problems such as drug abuse and violence coincide with a person's mental health and overall well-being. The transition from adolescence to adulthood can be a turbulent and confusing time for young people. Many adolescents seek a sense of belonging and fitting in somewhere or to some form of a group. That group of belonging can be with formulating friends or strong relationships in their family or home life.

Social and emotional learning (SEL) is the process through which children and adults acquire and effectively apply the knowledge, attitudes, and skills necessary to understand and manage emotions, set, and achieve positive goals, feel and show empathy for others, establish and maintain positive relationships, and make responsible decisions (Casel, 2021). Educators, parents, and policymakers who recognize that the core SEL competencies are necessary for effective life functioning also know these skills can be taught. Extensive research demonstrates that school-based SEL programs can promote and enhance a students' connection to the school, positive behavior, and academic achievement (Durlak et al., 2011).

> Classroom teachers can help students develop social and emotional competencies by using engaging curriculum materials and implementing specific instructional and classroom-management practices.

A school environment is ideal for developing social skills and mastering self-control while gaining a deeper understanding of how to self-regulate our emotions. Social-emotional learning can potentially be a catalyst in improving a student's decision-making skills, developing critical thinking and problem-solving skills. One of the aims of SEL is developing positive relationships in school among teachers, students, and their peers. After students can master SEL, these same skills or principles provide the opportunity for young people to become model citizens in the community.

CDC's Youth Risk Behavior Surveillance Data Summary & Trends Report: 2009-2019 highlights concerning trends about the mental health of U.S. high school students.

> - *More than 1 in 3 high school students had experienced persistent feelings of sadness or hopelessness in 2019, a 40 percent increase since 2009.*
> - *In 2019, approximately 1 in 6 youth reported making a suicide plan in the past year, a 44% increase since 2009.*

In addition, some children live in communities with poorly performing schools, and many families can't afford to send their children to college. The stress of living in poverty can also affect children's brain development, making it harder for them to do well in school. Interventions to help children and adolescents do well in school and help families pay for college can have long-term health benefits. Educational attainment can be used as a health outcome predictor. A person's education level plays a significant role in determining their potential income, and research shows that low-income individuals are often plagued by chronic health diseases. There are long-term ramifications of graduating high school and attending college, potentially improving health outcomes for minorities.

Social Norms

Social norms are commonly defined as the understood beliefs, standards, and behaviors of a group of people. On the community level, we must incorporate evaluating social norms to gain a better understanding of ways to academic success in underserved communities. To address the low number of minorities not completing a college degree program, we must take a closer look at how education is viewed in the K-12 grades and college years. Promoting academic success must be prioritized and embedded in the norms of marginalized populations. To address the excessive number of high school and college dropout rates of minorities compared to other ethnic groups, we must evaluate the level of importance of attaining an education in the beliefs and behaviors of minorities.

> It still takes a village to raise a child, and it requires a collective effort to promote the importance of attaining a high-quality education for all students.

The expectation level of academic success must be heightened throughout the community so that at-risk children hear about the value of an education at home, in church, at school, and throughout their local community. Community stakeholders must be intentional about promoting the importance of succeeding in school. Social norms encompass perception, and if students perceive that it is okay not to give their best effort in school, then the outcomes will not be favorable. Promoting education is a long-term investment that will boost the local economy when students return home after graduating college and begin to work high-salary jobs. Advocacy for the quality of education in minority communities must be a point of emphasis. Visibility with attending community events like city council meetings, parent-teacher associations meetings, or any public meeting event raising awareness for the need for more funding and resources for the local public schools. Active and vocal participation in the community provides the avenue to shift the social norms and misconceptions about the importance of education.

SECTION 7

Parental Role in Academic Success

Parental involvement is imperative for students to achieve academic success. With the advancement in technology, teachers are more accessible than ever via video conferences such as zoom, text messaging, social media, and utilizing email to stay informed about students' progress.

Three significant barriers prevent parents from becoming involved:

1. Time and life demands.

2. Lack of knowledge of specific ways they can help their children at home.

3. Various factors in the school environment.

There are three broad types of parent involvement: involvement at home, involvement at school, and homeschool communication. Communication is a key element that shapes parent involvement activities at home and school and enhances school-family collaboration. Effective communication between school and parents can be a determining factor in improving academic outcomes for students. Several factors affect the frequency and way in which parents become involved in their child's education at home and school and collaborate with schools. This section will first provide an overview of such factors and give parent and teacher perspectives.

Understanding Parent and Student Rights in the Educational System

When adverse situations occur at school, parents and children often feel powerless or voiceless. Parents feel forced to accept the recommendation that school officials hand down. Parents and students have a right to voice their concerns and express their points of view in educational matters. Parents and students must be provided a platform to ensure they are allowed a chance to articulate their concerns with school matters. The constitution of the United States gives each state absolute power to regulate its school systems. Parents and students must know the basic laws governing educational school systems in their state. It will be difficult to refute any situation if the parents and students do not know their rights.

School Counselor Role

It is essential to understand the role of a school counselor in the academic achievement process for students. One of the responsibilities of school counselors is to identify at-risk students and implement a plan to improve the outcomes for at-risk students. Typically, students are labeled "at-risk" based on the objection of failing to graduate high school. A percentage of "at-risk" students slip through the cracks without gaining the necessary skills to be academically competent on the college level. Some students can do just well enough to fly under the radar and never receive the individualized assessment of their cognitive abilities. The cognitive ability of students centers around how students receive and process information, including how knowledge is acquired, interpreted and retained.

Another important role of the school counselor is to provide academic advice to students. Students must have some input on their educational path. For example, a counselor may decide that a trade school may be more suitable for a student after high school. The student may not get the opportunity to be exposed to some rigorous courses that prepare students for college courses. In a situation like this example, students are denied the opportunity to aim for post-secondary education based on the opinion of the school counselor. Students should have a voice in planning for their futures. Students need the necessary tools and information that will help guide their decision-making process.

All students should become self-advocate and learn how to use their platform to speak up for themselves and become informed about issues that are relevant to their own lives. Students can become proficient in self-advocacy by researching topics that they are passionate about and becoming knowledgeable with evidence-based (credible sources of information), and effectively communicating their views on the topic to influencers and leaders. Self-advocacy allows students to conduct a self-inventory on the tools needed to succeed in school and life.

Parents and students should start preparing for college before the senior year of high school. They can begin as early as the ninth grade in gaining an understanding of the admission requirements for colleges and universities. I was one of those students that did not receive a lot of help around planning for life beyond high school and one of the motivating factors for this book. For the sake of the at-risk students that come from homes where the importance of education is not emphasized regularly, it is never too early to start planning for the future. Parents and students must be equipped with the information to make informed decisions about the student's future endeavors.

Parents and students should be proactive in understanding the laws governing their state and local school districts. Parents shouldn't wait until an incident at the school about their child before learning about the policies and procedures of the school district. For example, if the local school district issues a student handbook, I would advise all parents and students to read it. If the student handbook contains questionable information, it would be wise to contact school personnel as soon as possible and get answers to information that you do not understand. The Family Educational Rights and Privacy Act (FERPA) is a federal privacy law that gives parents certain protections concerning their child's education records, such as report cards, transcripts, disciplinary records, contact and family information, and class schedules. As a parent, you have the right to review your child's education records and to request changes under limited circumstances. To protect your child's privacy, the law generally requires schools to ask for written consent before disclosing any personally identifiable information to individuals other than you (U.S. Dept of Ed).

The Protection of Pupil Rights Amendment (PPRA) applies to the programs and activities of a state education agency (SEA), local education agency (LEA), or another recipient of funds under any program funded by the U.S. Department of Education. It governs the administration to students of a survey, analysis, or evaluation that concerns one or more of the following eight protected areas: political affiliations or beliefs of the student or the student's parent; mental or psychological problems of the student or the student's family; sex behavior or attitudes; illegal, anti-social, self-incriminating, or demeaning behavior; critical appraisals of other individuals with whom respondents have close family relationships; legally recognized privileged or analogous relationships, such as those of lawyers, physicians, and ministers; religious practices, affiliations, or beliefs of the student or student's parent; or income (other than that required by law to determine eligibility for participation in a program or for receiving financial assistance under such program).

PPRA also concerns marketing surveys and other areas of student privacy, parental access to information, and the administration of certain physical examinations to minors. The rights under PPRA transfer from the parents to a student who is 18 years old or an emancipated minor under state law (Student Privacy). A controversial issue primarily occurring in schools that consist mainly of minority students is a police presence in the school. In an equitable learning environment, police presence would mean providing a safer academic space, but on the contrary, statistics show that police are used to criminalizing black and brown students. Too often, disciplinary infractions that should be handled by school personnel result in the arrest of black students. This perpetuates the pipeline to prison problem plaguing black youth. Minority students are losing a staggering amount of instruction time due to suspensions. Data collected by the U.S. Department of Education's

Office of Civil Rights during the 2015-16 school year highlight the gross injustice and inequities of how disciplinary issues are handled in schools nationwide.

In far too many states, the loss of instruction experienced by Black students is often doubled compared to white students.

- In Missouri, Black students lost 122 days of instruction per 100 enrolled. There were roughly 145,000 Black students enrolled, and they lost a total of over 177,000 days of instruction in the state.
- Black students lost over 100 days per 100 enrolled in each of the five worst states for Black students: Ohio, Michigan, Mississippi, Tennessee, and Virginia.
- In each of these five states, Black students lost between 47 and 100 more days than White students.
- Tennessee and Virginia were also among the five worst states for students with disabilities. While this snapshot does not cover the confluence of race and gender, it is worth noting that while there are only 3.9 million Black boys enrolled in school, together, they lost more than 3.4 million

days of instruction due to suspension. That means that Black boys lost 86 days for every 100 enrolled nationally.
- Black girls lost 1.7 million days of instruction, or 45 days for every 100 enrolled. This is near twice the national average for all students. (ACLU.org)
- If you're stopped by a police officer at your school, stay calm. Don't argue, resist, run away, or otherwise interfere with the officer. Ask if you're free to leave. If the answer is yes, calmly and silently walk away from the officer.
- If the officer asks you a question, you have the right to remain silent. You also have the right to refuse to write or sign a statement. But if you waive these rights, anything you say, write, or sign can be used against you. And if you choose to make a statement, ask to have a lawyer, parent, or guardian present before you are questioned.
- You can refuse to give your consent to be searched by the police. This may not stop the search, but this is the best way to protect your rights if you end up in court.
- Don't consent to a phone search; police must have a warrant to search your phone.

The same goes for a strip search. No police officer or school employee has the authority to strip-search you.

- Don't resist, fight, or flee from an officer who is arresting you. Instead, say you wish to remain silent and ask for a lawyer immediately. Don't say anything, sign anything, or make any decisions without a lawyer present.

SECTION 8

Educational Strategies for Success

A mind is a terrible thing to waste. Next Level Educational Strategies (NLES) was designed to ensure that no student is left behind and prevent more students from falling through the cracks. For those students desiring to pursue a college education but do not know where to begin, we have compiled a list of proven steps to take control of their educational and career paths. Preparation is the key to entering college and succeeding in the classroom. Financing a college education can be a very stressful process. Next Level Educational Strategies is designed to meet any learner where they are in their educational quest, including high school students, GED program participants/graduates, and college dropouts with a desire to return to school. The motivating tools supplied in this book will empower students/parents to take ownership of their education and desired future outcomes. NLES takes you behind the educational processes and connects the dots to why particular tasks are essential to present and future educational success.

> "A key component to excelling in the classroom and life is gaining insight into the learning style category you belong to."

Students learn differently, and instruction should be tailored to meet the learning needs of the student. The mastery of subject content can be achieved in various formats, and learning is not a one-size-fits-all method. Knowing what works best for you as a learner will undoubtedly lead students to tap into their intrinsic motivation to exude higher self-esteem and willingness to invest in their future.

Learning style assessment exercise: https://www.gadoe.org/Curriculum-Instruction-and-Assessment/Special-Education-Services/Documents/IDEAS%202014%20Handouts/LearningStyleInventory.pdf

High School Years Checklist

Benjamin Franklin stated, "If you fail to plan, you are planning to fail." Students and parents alike should not wait until senior year of high school to start to map out strategies for life after high school. Courses taught in ninth grade are designed to prepare students to succeed in the tenth grade and so on until the completion of the curriculum for graduation. The same rules apply to preparation outside of the classroom for life after high school. Some steps can be completed each year of high school to ensure a smooth and successive transition to college. A high school checklist is a road map for students to strategically navigate tasks that should be completed by the end of each grade level in high school. Parental involvement is an absolute necessity for student success in school. A high school checklist is also a great tool for parents to be aware of what requirements should be accomplished by their child each year in high school. Below are some valuable resources for guiding parents and students through the high school years.

https://secure.edweek.org/media/131115-empoweringparents.pdf

https://www.pta.org/docs/default-source/uploadedfiles/k-june20

https://s3.amazonaws.com/rdcms-pta/files/production/public/Common%20Core%20State%20Standards%20Resources/2013%20Guide%20Bundle_082213.pdf (Parent guide for every grade level k-12).

http://www.centerii.org/techassist/solutionfinding/resources/PowerParInvolve.pdf

Parent involvement tips and resources:

https://www2.ed.gov/parents/academic/help/parentpower/booklet.pdf

More parent information on what students should be doing at various stages in K-12

What is Financial Aid

One of the most intimidating aspects of going to college is how to pay for it. Federal student aid comes from the U.S. Department of Education. It is money that helps a student pay for education expenses at a college, career school, or graduate school. Federal student aid covers expenses such as tuition and fees, room and board, books and supplies, and transportation. Students should be introduced to the realities of avoiding large student loan debt while financing their education. After completing college, my goal is that neither students nor parents are saddled with an insurmountable burden of repaying student loans. For many students, student loans will be the first line of credit that appears on their credit report post-college years. Student loans show up on credit reports as debt. An introduction to the world of credit rating and credit reports should be accomplished before enrolling in college. Applying for and receiving student loans automatically initiates the process of having credit report activity, so why not inform students of choices associated with Financial Aid.

There are three main categories of student aid:

- **Grants** – Grant money usually does not have to be repaid. Most U.S. Department of Education grants are based on a family's finances.
- **Work-Study** – Work-study money is earned by a student on or near campus while attending school and does not have to be repaid.
- **Student Loan** – Loan money must be repaid-with interest.

https://studentaid.ed.gov/sa/eligibility

https://studentaid.ed.gov/sa/types/grants-scholarships/finding-scholarships

https://fafsa.gov/

Applying to Schools

Many factors come into play when applying to colleges/universities. Below are some of the key factors included in the admissions process.

- Courses taken in high school
- Grades and overall GPA (Grade Point Average)
- Class rank
- Cumulative scores on standardized tests such as ACT & SAT
- Recommendation letters from school and community leaders
- Extracurricular activities, how well-rounded you are as a student
- Community service, displaying leadership characteristics

Students must be cognizant that the grades scored in each grade level of high school matter and will appear on their high school transcripts. What a student does in the 9th grade can play a role in getting into college or getting a job in the future. Many employers request high school transcripts as a part of the evaluation process before a job offer.

Volunteering in the community reflects maturity as well as leadership skills. Many scholarship applications inquire about community service(volunteering) and extracurricular experiences. Adding community service to a scholarship application will only increase the likelihood of getting selected for the scholarship.

One critical element in choosing a school is knowing the difference between accredited and non-accredited schools. Many students may desire to earn a college degree and eagerly enroll in an institution that knowingly offers worthless degrees because they are not accredited institutions of higher learning. It is a travesty for students to work hard to earn a degree and pile up a mountain of debt to the end of not landing a job because of where they chose to attend school. (https://www.ed.gov/accreditation

Financial Literacy

The leading cause of debt in America is student loan debt, further exacerbated by the underfunding of K-12 in public schools across the country. The teaching profession remains one of the most unappreciated and underpaid careers in the U.S.

The federal government and states invest the bare minimum for educating our students during the K-12 grades while allowing the student loan industry to prey on students of color and underserved students. After completing high school, teenagers face making adult decisions that will undoubtedly impact their lives after college. Before making difficult decisions such as applying for student loans, all students should be introduced to understanding the basics of financial literacy, including budgeting, money management, credit rating system, and understanding how their credit score will be affected by the choices made during the early adult years. Today, we are seeing more and more companies requesting credit reports during the hiring process. A bad credit score can be the deal-breaker in landing a great job or applying for a loan to purchase a home or automobile.

References

https://www.youtube.com/watch?v=IHEo1OeWVrI
https://www.youtube.com/watch?v=Hf4BgvN5f_E

https://www.bloomberg.com/news/articles/2018-10-17/

the-student-loan-debt-crisis-is-about-to-get-worse
https://www.theguardian.com/money/2018/oct/04/student-loan-crisis-threatens-a-generations-american-dream

https://casel.org/overview-sel/#:~:text=Social%20and%20emotional%20learning%20(SEL,maintain%20positive%20relationships%2C%20and%20make
(Cohen, 2006; Durlak et al., 2011; January, Casey, & Paulson, 2011; Kress & Elias, 2006; Weare & Nind, 2011; Zins et al., 2004)
https://www2.ed.gov/policy/gen/guid/fpco/brochures/parents.html
https://studentprivacy.ed.gov/faq/what-protection-pupil-rights-amendment-ppra
https://www.educationdata.org/public-education-spending-statistics#:~:text=Federal%2C%20state%2C%20and%20local%20

governments,of%20public%20education%20 funds%2C%20respectively.

AUTHOR BIO

JEROME faced many obstacles while growing up in an underserved rural community in Mississippi. He is a 2021 Harvard University Fellow deemed subject matter expert on Racism as a public health crisis. He developed content on the prestigious Harvard University digital learning platform (Lab Xchange) for high school STEM students worldwide, reaching millions of teachers and students. Jerome is a first-generation college graduate. Neither one of his parents attended college. He proposed that access and exposure to greater opportunities would provide at-risk students with the belief that they can achieve academically. He is a research scientist conducting cardiovascular disease research. He is currently a Ph.D. candidate in Public Health (Doctor of Public Health). He hopes to share proven strategies that have allowed him, once labeled an at-risk student, to achieve success at the highest level in academics.